Schoenberg in the Troposphere

Poetry

James Grabill

Cyberwit.net
HIG 45 Kaushambi Kunj, Kalindipuram
Allahabad - 211011 (U.P.) India
http://www.cyberwit.net
Tel: +(91) 9415091004
E-mail: info@cyberwit.net

Printed at Repro India Limited.

Contents

THE PRESENT HAPPENS TO BE 7
NO ONE KNOWS THE NUMBER 9
UNHEARD ROAR OF THE SUN 10
ELECTRIC WIND AND THE RAIN 11
AS THE WAR ON PEACE SPAWNS GAIA 12
GRANT WASHINGTON REPRESENTATION 15
THE ROAR DOWN THE ROAD 16
PIECES OF SHATTERED GUITAR 18
REMAINS OF VERACITY THAT REMAINS 21
REMAINS OF REVERBERATUM 22
WARNING 23
SHUFFLING A DECK OF MELTING CARDS 24
THE CRAWL WHERE WE GO 25
THE IDEA OF 2029 26
SURROUNDED BY THE MERGE 27
THE HEN'S MEDITATION 29
REDWOOD TEACHINGS 30
THE PAST PRESENT 31
WIND FROM THE COAST 33
THE NEXT DAY 34
SONG UNDONE 35

from Double Helix
　❋ What has already broken 38
　❋ The way birth left us modern 40
　❋ In the roaring of blast 42
　❋ The molten core 44
　❋ Faces out of the future 45
　❋ Sun branches through cells 47
　❋ Plants fired up 48
　❋ It turns out the crimson 51

❋ As if the future of the planet 52
❋ The custodian who moved here 54
❋ Miller and brown bomber moths 56
❋ You can sit for hours in the summer 57
❋ It may be a person will cry 59
❋ Each person here has suffered 61
❋ Wings lifting that fall 62

CITY LIMITS 65
THE IDEA OF AMPLIFIED GUITAR 71
READINESS 72
LIVE 74
UNEXPURGATED MAW 75
POETICS #41 77
SCHOENBERG IN THE PIN-DROP DARK 78
SOLIDNESS 79
DARK NIGHT 81
BLUE EAGLE 82
SIDEWALK VIOLIN 83
FIVE O'CLOCK SHADOW 85
GIANT SUNFLOWERS 86
THIS INSTANT 87
EVERY VOLUME IN STARLIGHT 88
SHE AIMS HIGH 90
HUNDERTWASSER PAINTINGS APPEAR 92
ZITHER 93

Acknowledgements 95
Books by James Grabill 98

I would rather have questions that can't be answered than answers that can't be questioned.

– Richard P. Feynman

The world is a complex, interconnected, finite, ecological-social-psychological-economic system . We treat it as if it were not, as if it were divisible, separable, simple, and infinite. Our persistent, intractable global problems arise directly from this mismatch.

– Donella Meadows

We are not made up, as we had always supposed, of successively enriched packets of our own parts. We are shared, rented, occupied. At the interior of our cells, driving them, providing the oxidative energy that sends us out for the improvement of each shining day, are the mitochondria, and in a strict sense they are not ours.

– Lewis Thomas

Every cell in the body has its own intelligence. Every cell in the body is functioning intelligently, much more so than your logical intelligence.

– Sadhguru

In nature's economy the currency is not money, it is life.

– Vandana Shiva

THE PRESENT HAPPENS TO BE

I.

For the present happens to be. With consequences in the paradigm shift this happens to be.

Model Ts putter over the steel bridge between centuries. And suddenly nobody's gigantic or small.

And everyone's so much alike that anyone in the future will have trouble telling us apart.

There could and should be room for all, enough water and food. If we were smart.

Should each moment fit into the whole? What happens is impossible to see without science and long-term contemplation.

Stay here longer. Too much will vanish if you go.

Replacing fire with electrical current is natural.

Heavy darkening reaches roots able to use it.

What moves ahead is this chance.

What should I change. What can I do? How do I make up for what I've received? How can I not try?

II.

Digits click through transience of self. Overworld waters alter further endangered species. Unknowing makes long moves of meaning quick as the flash of blood ties. Transcendental birth into arms of the mother has a little grip. And all things must fall in between.

As time goes on within eggshell memory, as molten as sleep is with waking, a century of advancement keeps waving goodbye to the old days driving off in the family Hudson which disappears with the grandchildren after rounding the green corner.

The next grains continue to arrive on a quantum slipstream, rewriting the effects of ignorance and its significant other, arrogance. At least around meal times this may be true. As working fingers and thumbs flip through months on their calendars, a great longing is triggered, for years when the hearth fires were burning, when innocence was more intact in the long days before discovery of microorganisms.

Flying over as we are, in these multiply-winged volcanically erupting neighborhood transport jets, who can say where we'll touch down next, in the midst of what conquest or abrupt colonization, what professional cotillions or bountiful flowerhead pungency, what usurpation or liberation?

Will we hear the human voice return in the midst of bell ringing or gourd shaking to say, *This is the place, the more-than-enough place, where you'll keep the fire and eat, where you'll wake and then sleep?*

NO ONE KNOWS THE NUMBER

It's raining and warmer in this part of the spectrum,
where money burns holes in those who live for it.
The tree in the body shivers in wind from Roosevelt
forests back through time. So who's in charge now
when the problem's what can't be privately owned?
Where isn't fresh water and rice a fistful of money?
So what is it we've done with our moths and birds?
After working all week, after this ongoing darkness
and incandescence, a person can end up saying,
Anyone who makes immense collections of money
has done so on the back of everyone and everything
else on Earth. Trusting the only hour here which is
and yet isn't a river of current arriving as it's leaving
can be a task. Unlearning predestination, a person
may ask, *Have I fallen asleep to what I once loved?*
Many fallen leaves blow through the mushroom soil.
No one knows how many people were planning to be
someplace other than this café of high noon and night.

UNHEARD ROAR OF THE SUN

We've never been here before, in the unimaginable
absent and present halves of the era feathering
off in glacial melts. Heaviness frames this exact
moment the more you study what could happen.
Still, those who were born today will imprint on how
it is, as if the place hadn't changed over our lifetimes.
For multiples converge in the roaring sun at the center
of cells, in the private maw, in the saucering galaxy.
Sun's torqued-up winds sharpen on the grinding wheel
of stars, as quantum force-field haloes from the Black
Madonna of Czestochowa emanate peace and sobriety,
mystery and possibility. If anything can pass through
another thing and still exist, it would happen in accord
with ancient Himalayan practices, appearing two places
at once as a surviving chance approximates the timeless
instant, which is here, and then gone. So it happens
ongoing thresholds of attraction and repulsion are
likely to admit more than enough for parasympathetic
reverberation of strings at the root of being awake.

ELECTRIC WIND AND THE RAIN

> But when I came to man's estate,
> With hey, ho, the wind and the rain…
>   - Wm. Shakespeare

This must be where the feet are
returning us to a dark room
on a moonless night, maybe to teach us
how little we know, how much
there is to learn about where and who
we are, as the information we're receiving
from the senses is unfortunately
limited, such as never detecting what was
swimming in a tall glass of water
until microscopes revealed it
as well as the cellular depths
and what seems to exist in matter.
We're still learning where and who we are,
surrendering before the unknown,
as the electrical brain recreates layers
and depths of the autonomous
and sacramental. For this must be
where the feet are taking us, as unfinished
as we are in Western civilization
with its sky filled with fire, slathered over
with stars and galaxies the longer
day passes through wires in the wall,
placing us in overlapping
fields of electromagnetic current
with the untested internet ajar.

AS THE WAR ON PEACE SPAWNS GAIA

Gargantuan coal-swollen 20th century furnaces still glow
hot white with spot-lit whitewashed mansions on the heights

with an eye on the expanse, where the latest climate
refugees must labor, pouring fresh vats of molten steel
along the monetary catwalk in the here and there

where high fashion wears towering women who walk it
before Ikegami flashes made in the anvil-oscillating
solar system carried by cosmic rays and gravity of this
octopus arm of the galaxy circling its black-hole drain
where the last surviving species has always been heading

wherever the earliest prayerful aspirations may have worked
spells to benefit the possible lot expanding exponentially,

to carry it further down the avenue of mounted antelope heads

telling us to begin where abstract expression on the wall
was pointing all this time, ever since the first sprawling
aspiration was launched under the raven roost cloud cover

in assumptions back in the gut where personal intent's moot

back in the collective as the scarlet carpet's nailed down
to conceal holes in the company floors in the face
of rank landscapes of the aesthetically impoverished
for whom the brain may not grasp what happened
to begin this chance to extrapolate from a few scraps

of evidence of the whole system that awards executives
bonuses for failing while directing undifferentiated
fury into labor negotiations from the underworld
forever dressed for morning in a sleek Italian bathrobe

on which figures taken from the Sistine Chapel ceiling
have been hand-stitched in gilt and wildfire threads

as if to wrench destiny loose from what used to be

civilization still around to answer questions,
as the lunar shadow in space slides its disk
between the sun and the other sun unseen

past every tipping point on carbon-fiber
Amazonian tail feathers that happen hot
in soul-speaking hues with dead-bolt accuracy

far from names, where we've got ourselves a situation
striking oil that floats in a film on gargantuan riches
for only a few spending all day in the monetary lounge

where nothing of the future could be blowing deserts
with punishing new storms, defying urgency
sharp as contemplation increasing uptake rates
of earlier parts of the independent human brain

with so little time it must have happened already

sure as shooting out of potholes of electromagnetic
x-rays potent with arterial halibut pitches in pungency
already modern as what begins moves a body out

through mortality fixing things good, sure as foregone

conclusions at the bare surface where people are
collected shoulder to shoulder in the ruby glow
of undeniable hunger in a Roman numeral countdown,

with archaic accord that exceeds ice-capped thought
which has traveled in long pitches through the build-up
of birth and unfinished carbonic breakdown to plunge

through unseeable air at every electromagnetic point
in slipstream 4-D used by the brain that keeps working
around the mind to harvest split-second resemblances

to safe passage in archaic Greek initiation rites
before a 6-foot pinecone that once gave young Greeks
power for the final transformation from childhood,

as feeling translates before dropping all it might own
on the casino table of identity still bearing up

under autonomous conscription not only of this

recent previous century but present capitalist
jibber-jabber arguing whether hunger encourages

the head to remain connected to the no-instant

with blood rubies in your face
in the dark where no one has been.

GRANT WASHINGTON
REPRESENTATION

Grant Washington in the District of Columbia
adequate representation in both houses.
Give Puerto Rico assistance and liberty.
Give redwood representation the hub of wheeling law.
Grant earthworms and crawlers tons of representation.
Grant Ulysses S. Grant Washington recognition.
Give aboriginal personhood to the first rivers you love.
Enact reparations for great grand sons and daughters of harm.
Give the imparting sea representation of depths.
Enact the sun rising into dawn of consciousness.
Grant the bride of anywhere-hunger her chance to swear.
Give meat its chance of animal sleep and eye-opening.
Hang the hats on meat hooks and give the dogs room.
Mammal the mother and father in little ones
with justice transacting personhood.
Give Washington its Grant and Puerto Rico drinking water.
Grant shelter from dark and light in a chance
as from burning cold and freezing heat.
Give foothills sheep their home on the rocks
and Washington adequate representation.

THE ROAR DOWN THE ROAD

That clamor out of the East, what's coming down the road, it sounds
    like the time ahead is made out of titanium with ten thousand
    gargantuan devices of trash collection rumbling
    on each future block fueled by inconceivable grief.
It's elephantine, the roar, more being touched inside out than hearing
    sound, a kind of cold current rolling like the ocean through rock
    of the planetary mantle then splashing out of the ground,
    countless speared pachyderms crashing down on their sides.
That roar, weather transformed by the ice melt in the air, magnificent
    animals fall crashing, great trees of forests in climax cracking
    in a booming thud on the forest floor, every original old-growth tree
    lost hundreds of times over erased in an instant without replacement.
It's the ocean sound of no replacement that attends death, one at a time,
    one gasoline explosion engine at a time and then the next,
    adding up to this racket, with every chain saw in Mississippi
    and Kansas buzzing, severing the habitat from its foundation.
Tens of thousands of sea lions in hollow rock coves, tens of thousands
    of big African cats locked in zoos, and tons of military donkeys
    are braying out of the Bible with propagation and suffering.
It's in a squall, this place by the road, where trucks are hauling secret
    ingredients to an invisible facility, as molten iron pours
    from taps until kitchens cave in to Iron Age crawl spaces.
Iron Age rhinos built out of iron must be charging down iron stairwells
    then bashing past the metal door at the bottom of the stairs
    to reach tens of thousands of electric guitars being broadcast
    from high-rise Fender amps for such intensity to be audible here.
Armies of liquified hillsides must be collapsing in bald mouths of scared
    ventriloquists shouting vacuous deafening blurs at the place
    where the sun sets, the Anthropocene braying, rumbling in mantle

from state to state, engines exploding, wrecking balls bashing
at remorse the shape of immense apartment houses buried in air.

PIECES OF SHATTERED GUITAR

Maybe no one shows up
to claim possession
of personalities of the deceased
waiving their rights to attorney
around reptilian maw on the radio
turned up hot from spikes
of emptiness when sea wings open
for those born to mothers before
all this TV army traveling on onerous
armistice rescinded for control
of flocks that blast into materialism.

All you need is love all you will not buy
with negotiations not for sale, not
until ritualized certainty steps in
with everybody following to the one
and only you've gotta love, to have love,
have warm love taking you to the place
where who knows if you need silent love,
connected love, connecting so you're able
to give love, when finding love, so you hear
the mind making moves electromagnetic
like no time before, any place we've been,
now that we're living in disrupted conditions
and what's most important is honest love.

So seeing-eye doors scan for exact matches
in the history of mapped faces, on the road
into emptiness heavy with machinery roaring

out of unstudied Gnosticism packing austerity
of the present era when redemption has work
to bargain over, given the number of sleeping
embargos flame-high in milks of the mammal
spectrum stone-serious about ethereal gravitas,
glass doors splitting open while the eye records
architecture of the human face, when something
gargantuan is trying to speak but finds no words
or reincarnation, just a sense of what could spill
off the planet, though lamas are saying chants
to benefit all sentient beings caught in the heat
and root-dark chills we see ourselves causing.

For breathing to be inextricable, the body knows
to individuate as one part of this living unity
where matter pivots at speeds of the leguminous
time it takes for liquid weeks to roll out of sight
while the Sphinx remains toothless around thirsts
at the fountain of peace keeping the big city alive
beyond arsenals, while the precipitous fall lifts off
the wild oceans in rolling waves that peak before
crashing through the pavilion of lions breathing
with bioluminescence down the path of solitude
if footsteps you take are your own simultaneously
particle and wave out of the moss-glowing green
prepared scripts for breath to be taken on by cells,
powering the transitory presence of being human.

Don't tell me you've just happened in
without history, or that people failed
to practice the Presbyterian pipes
for longer than this Jain enlistment
as brief as our immersion here is,

which swirls over the unseen deep
with hot and cold soundly mollified
and turned transparent on high,
where *one* refers to the collective.

REMAINS OF VERACITY THAT REMAINS

Responding to gravity						in the grip
of uncertainty

				maybe we were slow to notice
		where charged engines have burned
into mitosis,					after a catastrophic century

		had the glaciers melting over shipping-carton streets
	as tomahawk as home-grown jolts
		rife with pre-existence
				over unwavering cold-water sinks
					we've overheard from halfway down

in reciprocating old railyard lanterns
guided by the remarkable unseen
				in Celsius-laden forestry
		with dumped arsenic ash reaching valley-floor nerve

			in the swum-fierce underground
still beetling up or down in our conditions.

REMAINS OF REVERBERATUM

The air you're breathing
belongs to you more than to others

                    if only a few moments.

              Therefore, I persist in my long-held belief
              that matter in the world remains solid.

The consequences of craving
cracked into   allow nuclear nation-states
                  to go unspooled in negative positives

from hip-lashed floundering flat-out crowning within winds blowering
wilderness pickerel in conscription haunted ragged by jaguar remnants,

speaking of word from the cradle in a dinner bowl wild card's chance
to fall soft on pungent Azorean breezes out of pollinated Teutonic hymns,
to stand what boot steps flatten.

                 That is, as small as the voice
of the self may be, if nothing much needs to be said about dying in full,
from overexposures to hope,   why not establish residence

in what brought us here   out of stillness
with its sacred trust   that invented transformation

when nothing became something,
when something was perceived?

WARNING

This warning may contain unexpurged
forward thrust liable to burst pipe
organ tiers out of protestant pinecones
swollen with amotorized replacement
ground-mowing parts, acetylene blanched
ahandle in amnesic high court marshes.

Associated exploit-dirging may run plush
with Etruscan crowed airs as has been
physician-observed and judged justified
in immaculate sling tailing anaconda
gone armless from the era before words.

This warning may bleed without notice
in gongs at face range if held yonder
as balks cognito buttered stained-glass
Freud PR yearning through tit busts out
leopard-paused magna cum obsidian ruby.

Noticed may be further inside conception
with a lotta later-day perched doves
that dive head-long into the fermented
protectorate hrah gestating in untoward
Magna Charta with oyster-floor Bertha
roasting in a bed that promulgates
fluorescent flow joints flowering skirts.

SHUFFLING A DECK OF MELTING CARDS

At the door, wanting credit for whole periods of history
are numbers of characters we met in grammar school,
back when learning eclipsed understanding. Suddenly
who knows what ferocity and sweetness have undergone
refinements instantaneous as salmon-swim hope, explosive
as the guillotine drop of mountain-top memory suspended?

As this time wheels on thin ice and equatorial tiger tongues,
doesn't every moment race ahead of its locomotive weight
to reach the ancestral house where the present consists
of readiness and is forever launching away from extinction.

So molecular engines of polar abrasion enwrap the Antarctic
with promises, while the feathered dinosaur cultures loom
under tropical fractal streams unfolded in the spectra of risks.
In the nerve-center sky, light reverberates as the cells work
on the brain, adapting it for the latest pressures from matter.

It's clear little about people and air could have been different.
But the present hasn't surrendered, for nothing's inevitable
where nothing's been. What lifts the blood searches in space
for signs of life, as half of the clockwork day remains night,
and night still includes esoteric kinds of Bodhisattva mystery.

Through emptiness and catastrophic courtesy, self-organized
weavings of intricate microorganisms, shoulders of elephants
and the sea otters, the cells reach from the root for precision
that has given the compass its point and up-rocked artistry,
its corn-splashed yards of sunlight and eye-going instant
of collective origins, as the unconditional genome overflows.

THE CRAWL WHERE WE GO

For the long day's flooding across parking lots and the plains,
absorbing milestones and the smaller towns, coyotes loping
along the edge of belief and bridges suspended across rivers
linking hemispheres of a city, sunlight prisming through dew
on cables as if they were vibrating with chords no one's heard,
swamping glass towers with egalitarianism between the species.

Still, calibrated wealth-bought hurling-out vehicular Detroit
was held secure all night under smoldering sodium pentothal
security lights casting their pall of milky maw that rescinds
Zoroastrian calendars all legal-like for solar parallel familiars
retrofit for urgency with concentration on wealth as a sport.

Call this Detroit, where either you pay big for water or lose it,
or The Towers of Ambrosium, land of manufactured miracles
as wealth touches lightning to instantaneous pneumatic tubes
delivering money up to the head office where the vacuum's safe
in glass, with no impoverished arms reaching in a locked factory
for the red and black master switch, with no adopted paratactic
restlessness roaring when death climbs the ladder from the Aztec
palace with its gold flasks loaded for the trajectory into nothing,
nothing above the hard rungs of the ladder, nothing to see below.

For this is the crawl of the garden spider, weaving into gusts
on a break from swallowing 100s of years of children's winter
with tens of thousands of ballistic ministers blazing in pulpits
decrying sins on a dark Mobius night in which fertility primes.
And this is the photo-electric nightcrawler reaching across dirt
to touch another, to secure the down-dwelling lift of the future.
As we live, we're held by waves expanding from all that's here,
what happened over our lives, and much we could never know.

THE IDEA OF 2029

Classical ambition will stand behind and in front of an espresso counter. A conversation will spike up under '50s band shells of old assumptions, that the new world never ends and no number of kids would be overdoing it.

Counter-intelligence satellites will direct more off-world parabolic dishes toward street-corner spreads of rumor-mongering in speculative cosmology, as mystery and natural wildness disappear further with flora and fauna from before Earth was peopled.

Before the church married its own establishment, priests may have been hearing a single-skinned shaman drum through the wall. Seeking strength, they practiced chanting the invisible closer, hoping to live more fully, calling the sense *home*, and they still will.

Coffee cups will be refilled, where long-term discussions continue on their own steam. Blue potatoes will be spaded up somewhere behind brick apartments. Split-middle willowing will swim with the truck of civilized yields., Baseline torque from where the oil-lamp right whales dropped will still leach into love and fear.

More than ten years will pass in an avalanche of melting ice, rewriting the encyclopedia. Presence won't be the only human effect in all the blinding blue blazes taken for granted. The next era will feel sorry for this one, thirsty and hungry enough as it is, in small rooms where anyone has been.

SURROUNDED BY THE MERGE

Who need be afraid of the merge? – **Walt Whitman**

What provides the human body lift, as we move
and rest, rises up in the cells.
Vivid pulchritudinous tail feathers remind us.
Intuiting the presence of further possibility
has been a sense within us.
The impulse to stand here, to employ the eyes
to look up into star-burning night,
searches through space for signs of life.

A young clerk whose name is Philobus talks low on the black telephone
of the '50s, as humanity proceeds nonstop, driven forever to drive faster.
Typhooned electrical sutras keep researching live states of contempla-
tion. Matter doesn't stop or go, but waits for the nuclear flash to never
happen. It could be the day of the snake back in the stone canyon with
the river

for a nanosecond ignited by profuse light
on the blue terrestrial shell
that over time filled with being.
Under the inconceivable starry canopy of galaxies,
people learned how to trust the drift
and wheeling, to let honest words arise
so thinking doesn't collapse in squealing
groans of twisting steel bridge beams

while the train slithers ahead on its pilgrimage under the starry canopy
of gargantuan numbers visible after dark. It might be about time to

realize the shame in our faces would be our own, as the engines aren't
humming, but thundering with explosions. So choosing what to do or not
to do burns as sunlight falls through large numbers separating actors
from their acts

> where consciousness rests on thought,
>   as thought takes consciousness
>   back in a nanosecond to light
>   the Earth's blue shell into being.
> This is the place where the raven mask opened.

THE HEN'S MEDITATION

A hen in her prime out back recognizes where her food comes from. She's no idiot, and usually close to where the chicken-keeper scatters it.

Maybe she's grateful, but her duties engage her. Alert to the order around her, if she's not in a cage, her brain takes her on walks for a little education in the barnyard. Her role is to assume her position, as a protected mother whose responsibility reaches beyond her.

As the rooster crows and time flies, the hen largely sits where she belongs. Planets orbit and eggs appear. Perhaps she speaks up, but mostly she's practicing meditation she picked up as an exotic feathered nun alert for orbs within her care.

A delivered egg occurs to her while she releases it, sounding her voice that the present's sinking its root, which means the rooster keeps pushing. He can't let the perimeter go or have a chicken missing. It's tenuous, urgent, the continuing invention of social order which gives a chicken meaning.

If one of the kids enters the coup to collect eggs, a hen with her weight and warmth set over what might in her meditation begin to hatch may decide to stay put.

Aware of the kid, the hen may look off, to conceal more of her presence. Maybe the kid will disappear and not her egg, not the center of her ambition, which, as long as it's under her, exists outside the present time.

REDWOOD TEACHINGS

For over two years, Julia Hill lived at the top of a 200-foot old-growth redwood through Northern California winter up there and hot summer, through Pacific storms with extra wind, after one of the logging tycoons bought the right to take what he wanted, paying the low price for lumber, not the high value of keeping carbon out of the sky.

For over two years, climbing branches 170 feet up early in the morning, giving herself to the tree she named Luna, she survived, and so Luna stood. Teams smuggled in what she needed, where woman and tree were rooted, with Basho and Issa nearby, maybe Snyder and Oliver not far off when she could see great cribs of morning light shuddering alive, green lifted out of ground by root.

Trees are our teachers, a Seneca elder has said. *We follow the history of Earth, whereas other cultures follow the history of mankind.* On good days, I think I know what she means. Today is a good day, and clearly Earth is the mother of blue jays and all the aspen and brown ants, the mother of all mothers and non-mothers, and look at us—mostly not even speaking her language yet.

Before the Civil War, Emerson spoke an internal-external waking-up and sleeping syntax of beings, minerals, and plants for a while, seeing nature as *exponent* of who we are. On a good day, I know something of what this meant, cubed by rustling tall grass, or raised to the sixth power by a raven softly cawing over the trail, or touched to a fourth by a round squirrel, expanded to an exponent of wind and wooden guitar played by a neighbor in the summer afternoon behind the houses.

But then it all must come to dust, as the Cymbeline song goes. The lovers part and then Earth rolls past them like the click of a shutter, the camera of universe filling Emerson's mind a moment with oceanic beautiful unity, like hearing Estonian brass in a Pärt symphony relive the massive turning of experience into honesty.

THE PAST PRESENT

I.

Evening that murmurs with consequences of centuries of learning has its instantaneous winds arriving from other towns in daylight, in the fossil atmosphere, at the beginning of the end of long fires.

The widening pulsation that splashes through the center of the world is everywhere, growing in complex prayers for relief, being loaded on docks losing paperwork sheet music to the other sides of sun, in the braille hiss of pipe-blistered needs, in heave of long-standing ache, from the days we lived on branches.

For we've lived with cardinal words of bearing from old fathers and mothers.

With crimson feathers of the body of dusk.

Around black leathers squeaking in half-lit rooms.

Along liquid neural avenues delivering from way back.

Where the half of your life you can't sell will keep you alive.

II.

Future seawater rises come down with rain, pounding more holes in the continuum. Breathing in which sunlight turns on cellular disposition revolves on immensity and the slightest shifts of sync. But won't the whole be delivered to parts, when fractal multiples advance?

The future calls out from the vanishing point where everyone meets. Streaming fronts pour, torqued around the planetary horn. Mud-spattered medieval armor crashes to the floor. The past's been subdivided, when what could be other than collective?

We can see lateral distributions of centralized power trading destinations and subtropical slurries of momentum. Mindfulness extends us from long lines of mothers and fathers, which in no time become different or the same.

On downtown walks, the early brain may well burst awake, in what could be a remnant of mammalian birth. Whatever working cells select, we've been given a chance to sleep determined to wake. Opposites circle one another the moment weight kicks in.

The distance between two people alive who once were together can be measured—in the time it takes one to realize the other exists, as a kind of wave washes over.

WIND FROM THE COAST

The fresh air that lifts can be far from land
with no word for the place where it's risen,
its buoyancy a kind of parachuting away
from the planet, where the moment's a flash
of warmer air pressed into a lip of the cold
over choppy shrimp-stained waves that ride
on squid-shot depths expelled by upwelling
restlessness, the wind forced into a nonstop
search for nothing specific in a rushing limbo,
forced into banishment from incomprehensible
short-faced heaves that keep the air shaking
up what it reaches, as if the place were never
good enough or *there's no time like today*,
where the wind's lost, never at home, always
being dismissed, burrowing through emptiness
into the future, maybe disgusted by matter,
the wind, forever bound to run into it here,
spreading and then swirling, sliced sideways
and converging, crashing wherever it goes.

THE NEXT DAY

So it's the next day and we're still alive on the planet out of which we were pieced together and made for, on which we've thrived beyond overflow capacity and immersed ourselves in a collective mutually interdependent culture propped up by the evolved species and mineral sense.

With all the fasting and ascension, the retooling of Arctic winds around wooden guitars to be held for the hog-blinking duration, through certain rains we've inherited, we've received of course an amount of species arrogance pieced together before science when much was impossible to explain and magical thinking reigned.

And yet this is the chance we were given, to live while the clock hands wheel and numbers vanish along with the sky eventually darkening, where heads of the sunflowers eventually bend heavily toward the ground, as if sizing up where their seeds will fall.

Unfinished presence extends, where mushrooms stake out reclamations.

Stitches Grandma made to dresses on her seamstress bodices I'm sure still exist where they were drawn with attention taut, right for the mother with a baby in her arms, in the room behind the door that stays closed.

SONG UNDONE

You may already be a pungent tropical breeze
  the colors of an Amazonian parrot.
You may be uranium executrix for the grievously mindful.
You may already be a moth inventing your own form
  of transformation, or believe nothing
  much needs to be said about dying,
For the cells of the wildest grasses will speak, call it,
  with human cells in interspecies sense,
  before standing alive with solidarity.
No snow-white absentee society glistens within sight
  while heavy water burns out of history.
No aboriginal incendiary clock claws apart the familiar
  exotic emptiness and fullness in being alive
  that co-evolves, but slowly enough to not be missed
  in an eyelash pulse or a mayfly's slight digestion.
Without gas in your cosmic cylinders for hours on the road,
  would your loaf even conform with shape?
Would we know what was on Chaplin's Alaskan table?

The untelling handiwork of your own terse regret without rock
  of the coast over your shark sloughs swimming
  makes dark benedictions for strains of Intelligentsia.
But who wants to risk sabotage of our known antigravitational
  treble up-hammered into high rat-squeal urgency
  before the spectacle of the greater osmotic undone?
The brain proves it is an extraordinary stringed instrument
  that pursues a medium of echo-location in reverse,
  liberating day from automated xylophone backdrops.
For no coal cat's dark skulk comes bearing embryonic depths

of communal joy. No amniotic sways of unfound
fractions must breed in cavernous caresses
past the truck-wrecked milks in prayerful craving.
For waking-sleep positions the self in two locations
at once, upon the fluid planetary balance
and rigorous nerve in contemplation,
for a view standing apart from the world.

from Double Helix

It is raining DNA outside. On the bank of the Oxford canal at the bottom of my garden is a large willow tree, and it is pumping downy seeds into the air. ... [spreading] DNA whose coded characters spell out specific instructions for building willow trees that will shed a new generation of downy seeds. ... It is raining instructions out there; it's raining programs; it's raining tree-growing, fluff-spreading, algorithms. That is not a metaphor, it is the plain truth. It couldn't be any plainer if it were raining floppy discs. — **Richard Dawkins**

❋

What has already broken
off from usefulness
whirls up in yellow-gold marigold
pollen floating over North
American nightcrawlers glistening
with mud of feather fiber and eggshell
mayfly carcasses, the cross-mingled
lichen and white hair with molecules
in jurisdictions of the unseen,

the disintegrated baby cough
fresh water, the shaken-off
heavy museums of violet outskirts,

the root of sense at the ground
of the world, honey bees imprinted
on origin, peppering of tribal

calculus on road signs every so
often, the downsized next place
with mile-high crow wing
open-bloomed night sky.

Through exhalations, prejudicial
appeals the hour makes
have their blue jay feathers

that grow along nerve
as the young maple has spread

branches more apart in the blue

bowl of unfinished hours
that make room in back

so the flowering ovum
turns into sweetness.

✸

The way birth left us modern
in this era, dead-center,
breathing and long into the story
of health, with unities and divides
where matters have been ending
in the current, where findings
are still just arriving,
                    rains reach
the cells, and roots sink as the sky
flies over torch-lit laboratories
of the unconscious, simple as coal.
Hasn't enough clear-cut extraction
gone on already, restless and inverse
as nudity is, compared to the mind

now in the midst of mapping Earth
for microbiological populations
as evolved in topsoil and stallion,
smallest antennae and ant lion,
with white oak trunks assembled
out of fractions lifted in rings
within rings of the whole?

How smooth the lake can be
days before a storm, or hours
preceding shifts in the species,
as strengthen the red-brown
in a finch feather constructed

here out of rain and mineral
soils, steadied by the mammoth
past, with herds that painted
themselves onto first rock
in caves where the fire was,
then later into savannah.

✱

In the roaring of blast
furnaces still of 19th century
assumptions, fuming overhead
where conveyor drive axles scrape,
squealing from the works, the belief

in subservience especially of unlike
others, the warehouse forests and hills
seen for the taking in darkness
of day, where antique torque reaches

for lips and the private jaw, in the rise
and fall, to be delivering any fresh
upwashes and iterations of symmetry
over and above any longer-term procreative

presence as may arc over, multiply
conceived or not within the complexity
of stallion lines in a face, crimson-clear
nuclei in the churns, the ongoing
transnational externalizations of spoils

as leave behind mathematical avalanching
brightness of melting antiquity, the stone
thighs losing focus in fast-forward brushes
with the invisible prairies in each molecule,

then with hydrogen prophecy as it has been
wailing from the North Atlantic breakers
where buoyancy stops, filling in from the root,
what lifts with the cardinal compass periphery,

wheeling in Himalayan sky from far back,
the brilliant yogic healing at dawn
with its wing of dust from cries
along tracks of the absolute

risk, not only for the lyred
Majorcan angels going silent,
after uncertain prediction
out of dreamtime Celsius
as in Anchorage which has rocked
on a skull of magma, in a ruins
toward the end of global extraction,
where undersea Tetons are still
taking a further chance
on their moths' wings.

❋

The molten core of biological necessity
emptying to be filled
the razor-edged findings of slow-motion curves of cheekbones
the kindness and sad cases vaporizing in a walk to the car
the arcing draw of integers and brown-rice taste of sunlight

the gyres of cellular knowledge transacting their cross-pollinations
the hourly newborn interweaving of sense of ancient grandfathers

the swarthy sweat-scented abstraction, intelligent opposable thumb
the interspecies genetic conventions of mammal mothers of mothers

the flashing crack of another eggshell sentence suddenly no longer

the star-necked general chalkboard beholden to the defenseless
the hankering for horse-cart boiler-making current public trust

the leaves rotating on branches breathing into us and out of us

the interwoven energy and efficiency worked into solid strategy
the antiquity of uncountable acts peopling the place of existence

the arcing draw of night along a few thumbprints of vanishing sky.

❋

Faces out of the future
generation in a flash
can show up in the street

windows of the house
of knives, in downtown soup

spoons and baby-blue neon
Pabst scrawl burning in primordial
embers of their long past

furnace flames. Like a dozing uncle
on a dark afternoon of water,
magnetic resonance haunts
the gravitational moss-haired

stone walls in the gorge
close behind us, and before us

as regulated work days wash
sleep with their gardens
and tower bells rust in metallic
equations, the bare bulb
hung from the ceiling of atoms.

The offshore roiling boom, broom
of sweeping afternoon strafes
and composes through industrial
corn rows, the yellow-orange white

sunlight in hallways of ears,
the clear blue bowl
of the pre-Cambrian

in the yard, the sun of hard
old corn in hairy joists
and lumbered
trunks of family.

❉

Sun branches through cells
in almonds and shade,
as through the shock of hips
caught in a soundless ring
of mud-caked Ice Age bells

or muscular Brazilian canopies
dragging out their disappearance.

When quickening heel clicks echo
in marble basements downwind
from anyone's vaults of lessers and betters,
the stealing away in night-blinding muds
commences. Ennui polices socioeconomic
succession with flat-out torque
at the core of coal-swollen externalities.

Agility sways, as deep blue intensifies
behind blood-bearing flags that followed
Magellan around the global horn.

Feathering off melts in the saucering galaxy,
in an overflow is root heart heat in a roar.
Where hard-wired displays of impermanence
shatter around animals from before words,

the blue bowl holds open
for steaming soups,
or the brush of tiniest
mineral ribs of a cell.

❋

Plants fired up in global churns and on downslopes,
in light of soaks in the cradling of lathered-up split-middle
space turned Mayan-yellow where the new world never ends

in arcing blank-slate fertility,
unphenotyped, plummeting at edges
of sky-burned coal, in the long practice
of abandonment, with extended hours
that evening then return for the history
of 1000s of religious sects separated
from the whole, in the open stretches
of nothing to do that should or shouldn't be done

in all-solemn parallel cuffs, the terpsichorean sluice
converging in boilerplate Celsius in this Anthropocene Era

with insinuations of lift in the small ribs of a feather,
the peel of continuum around the north tundra
bubbling with methane, what the 7 to 8 billion need
from umbilical torque and sense of Old English,
in view of foreign purchase of African farms
or White House rooms in the drop of a scarf,
jangling earrings blended under safety lights
with brilliance of galaxy Markarian 231

dwarfed by slams of business cards onto velvet gaming tables
pasted over with photos of industrial waste sites,
abandoned towns given back to North China,

the extenuating honey hive brushes with emptying
to be filled at the lip of reinvented dives

in detachment, with subsensory pulse breeding
exceeded expectation and the up-birded
driving absent or present in body-to-body waves
erasing up-and-down seawater depth,
needle-eye gusts threading ferns that comb
through the air in fir forests for days within days

thickening with propagation that swims in a drop
of extenuated rain, jet engines screaming over raw sinks,
the molten core of biological necessity
with razor-edged findings of slow-motion curves
of cheekbones, kindness and sad cases
that vaporize in a walk to the car,
the arcing draw of integers and brown-rice taste
of sunlight from gyres of cellular knowledge
transacting their cross-pollinations, the hourly newborn
interweaving of sense of ancient grandfathers, the swarthy
sweat-scented abstraction, intelligent opposable thumbs,

the interspecies genetic conventions of mammal mothers of
mothers,
the flashing crack of another eggshell sentence suddenly here
no longer, the arcing draw of night along a few thumbprints
of vanishing sky, the legacy of overheard violin downtown
in the Oregon summer, Zoroastrian stellar bursts
of long-standing dynamo Ginsberg, breathing cells
of skin seen in the last amber of locomotive lanterns,

the lit directional brilliance of ground-dwelling territorial bees,
the enmeshed papal encyclicals that leached into love and fear,

countervailing flugel horn fugues that accompany ripe Sousa,
the stretch of muscular agility that feels what in a goose step,
the surviving edge that roars with a forest of lumens in cells.

All this seems to have emerged once people in corn-yellow
masks ascended the solar stairs, around construction and collapse
of time each moment they couldn't waste, where blue intensified
behind medieval pounding rains into which imperative rode
while old drums mushroomed by morning mostly from nowhere.

For winds moving through wormholes will gain further losses
given back to soils that sweep in through nuclear space
with forgotten capacity, accompanied by sad vestiges
of little-understood privatized communion
under rudimentary choirs of giant firs
sounding out for the Earth into distant space,

germinating quickness, with rash tresses in rock of the cells,
the praying mantis behind its mask, far back in light of the cells.

❋

It turns out the crimson chest can be torn by the look on a face,
by a painted moth that flies in the city center unknowing
with opalescent jellyfish parachuting in blood-bone slowness,

as through spreads of spider-thread air with circulatory hunger,
storms building that transmogrify salt-sea neural headwaters,

long shifts of cathedral vastness entering a few candlelit rooms,
around occult nerve within intangible wheeling through starlight,

as by more Roman numerals losing their long-term animals,
rapid extrapolations that descend within the hold of dark,
flashes of brilliant Arctic ice-face calving within immensity,

or sprays that cedar a human voice in lamp-quick hemp shades,

the sundown sliced into hemispheres in the world of principle,
the look in red howler eyes looking down from solid branches,

by future electromagnetic piano keys a few people may recognize,
evenings that exist in meteoric rain forests of ascending art,

in the safe-keeping of translucent womb-warmed neural rhizome,
slow-motion fern-combs that mushroom out under breathing,

with the winds on a sea roof, where mind sleeps before knowing,

and overlooked convergence absorbing the blue old future,

or willingness of the human species to sacrifice beauty,
as by Arctic auroras that move in on energy of a wing pulse.

✸

As if the future of the planet
had become cloaked
by scientific prediction,
after it had been hijacked
by fanatics, as if the nearby future

had fallen into slumping hypnotic stillness,
the way mid-day sunlight strikes
an abandoned and sealed-over nuclear plant—

the city seen where its future left it for the night
with its avenues glowing streetlights
as if they were its only valuables, luminous,

in spheres of medieval vapors the shiny
fabric of the robe a woman slips carefully off
her shoulders and away from herself,

placing it half-folded near the end of her indoor pool
with inlaid Moroccan tile few others,
if any, will see in the blue light she uses

when swimming back toward her family in 1970,
when the dollar drove people further
and the family business tripled,

its thunderstorm over flat Nebraska
with sudden night lightning flashes

cracking hollow in people's chests expanding,
collapsing, opening with the sky

into how the business
used to feel like being
in a brilliant up-wheeling

but later, she's seen business
is slow, after so much transpired
through the years

and some had gone, looming
off in a flash
into slow whiplashing,

and some had died
into an empty sanctuary
for a god that children
and older people fear like hell
the older they get
and the closer they feel

to being struck by a bolt,
when both body and resolve
will have been ignited
to the infinite
horizon, leaving
the world long gone.

❋

The custodian who moved here
from Estonia hauls the iron
gate to the floor and locks it down.

He looks at his wrist as skylight dampens
the white banquet tables with late afternoon
light.
  A woman in her yellow raingear
stumbles, continuing, notebooks in her arms,
Celsius rising, national mineral rights
claimed by individuals, with the commons
largely ignored around so much eating,
partaking, meeting up on Saturday evening
in throes of erotic propensity,

  the written word and small animals
teaching people, even the starved seabirds
in the Pacific found dead, stomachs packed
with plastic pieces of toys and devices.

      It turns out not long ago we were more in sync,
when topsoil wasn't blowing off in clouds
so often and we'd never have guessed we'd know
now that our coastal cities will be going down
in seawater heaves, in sea waves swollen
with wing-beat beauty and ground-down ruby

salts of spleens, soaks of penciled-in Bible pages
with tribal membranous slaws of paraphernalia,

the feral legal milk-dusts, in the green smoldering
sea-sluice of front-counter molds to the root.

It turns out we're growing mass
migration on land as the sea withdraws in rips
then pummels infinitesimal soups
in the airborne burn of honeybees
washed out, until you tell yourself,
*Go on, grieve for the future, work
where you are, work and wait.*

❋

Miller and brown bomber moths
of all dispositions used to cling
to the front screen all evening.
The dance floor was packed
with fluttering and quiet fluting,
as if wind had thrown them in
sideways and head-first straight
to the buttery glow of rural electrification.
Before high-propriety chemistry was exacted
on the complexity of soils and Orwell's *1984*
had been taken as a manual for spin
giving exploitation a friendlier face,
the moths used to gather, some of them
hurling themselves in and bouncing
off the screen, fired up by this
short life into urgency, lithe
and awkward, flung to the wire
by darkening, in what could only
have been hunger and the will
to survive. Where are they now
in the evening? Who can be sure
even of her own direction,
when a door has blown open
in the sky from the fault
of *All this is yours*?

✸

You can sit for hours in the summer
by the red blossoms in back,
near the blackberries that grew
through, and still miss seeing her.

She may have spotted the red
in the distance, and watched it go
almost ultraviolet, drenched in sunlight

in the immensity, before she flew in
from the nest she made earlier,
by tying strips of tall grasses and debris

into knots with her beak, fixing them
with spider filaments, then padding
the bed with lichen. And yet it's sudden,

when she shows up at a flower, drinking
red, and in a flash already she's
finished, her body pivoting mid-air,
as if she weren't doing anything

making the sound you can't hear
as much as sense within the chest,

the hum of her invisible wings,
a shudder nearly gone in the ruins

of light, the whole of her turning
emerald, into a piece
of ceremonial jewelry
escaping the Pharaoh.

In time, she flies in as she has before,
and faster than trying to see her
living at the speeds she does, already
she's gone into the vulnerable

atmosphere, having left behind
everything in a color
the opposite of hers.

❋

It may be a person will cry
before beauty in a final chord
follows the furious slides
through intricate half tones
and unfolding tunes of more
than could easily cultivate a resolution
of the gravity and light, slathered quick

with a painter's knife before rounding off
at vanishing points, the moment
a pole-vaulter's slung to the back
of common oxygen and forgets
her strengths and weaknesses, her latest
and old, when pivoting up, mid-air,
approaching the bar as more than a body.

A split moment must exist, that thrives
beyond argument, in the common intensity
of labor, the next person's shoulders
that glow in the sky, the brilliant light
that showered us at birth, as sense detected
for intelligence of the cells. If only for a stretch,

seeing that light must have been enough,
as beauty takes little away and leaves behind
circulation, wherewithal which has fallen
silent before beauty, though we know
the poor will be looked at raw then ignored,
the way poverty makes people more vulnerable
and subtly reflects on those with enough.

But a dancer can choose to walk on her feet,
projecting her solid shoulders to those
with shoulders, where seeing speaks to cells
the moment a person's moved, whether crying
may have quietly collected—will it matter

after the facts have stopped their requests,
after the blue jay has landed in energy
to eat what remains on the ground
then returned to the embassy of trees?

✳

Each person here has suffered
a loss that broke at a depth,

when he or she was taken
away from parts of the self,

as when we were taken at first
from the mother, when oneness

was forced to condense in the cool
white room. Perhaps after being

placed on a steel table or scales
that started in with their gravity,

the first breath could kick in
the way it was burning through

the whole body breathing light
in a room. Could the unconscious

drive forgetting or give comfort
to the whole underground mind?

Where cells have bent through
longing, in waves of the whole

risk of this place, won't the first
forces be working ahead to heal?

At the integrity of shape, light
turns away, but only parts leave.

❋

Wings lifting that fall
in thermals and arcing heaves,
single hours of sky that avalanche
in streaming light from mesas
and peaks to the heart of matter
and chance, the seen and unseen
heights that garden facts on the ground,

for the mind falls with sunlight lifting
in wings that thicken with precision
in between openness and shuddering
propulsion behind the genome of forgiveness

for whatever failed to work or has been epidemic,
fogged out, or what opened up along impulse
before drawing back, retracted for a landing,

as the current seven-heading-to-eleven billion
will sleep and then wake, sleep then wake,
each birth into longing that begins in cells,
where it ends, as light and dark swallowing
what happens or never came to be.

      Living light has let us witness
through lapses and stands what balances
within bearings, where palaces have been

built out of capability and stay maybe
a handful of years before what was forgotten,

unknown, or far from sync bears down,
the wings morning and evening taking on
the current light in long-term alignment
of the instrument of adaptation,

the adjustment of intensity
in cellular discovery
that goes on beneath
this life in the practice
of intrinsic worth
of interlinked species.

CITY LIMITS

I. The City Sleeps and Wakes

The modern city unregulated
in a state of overflow hires
a variegated staff before it sets sail
on a black Steinway with the sheen
of a spinner dolphin taking aim
for where the sun goes sinking dusk
fast into the ocean of microorganisms,
for the city if it were a person revels
in looming amounts of raw conflict
and joy if for no other purpose
than to see it's survived in presence
long enough to recover from work,
then fall asleep in the arms of water
one bird to the next, one last or first
cigarette flicked into a cereal bowl
before a beriddled city in climax slips
off its handle in heavy floods, in solar
spotlight which overtakes crossings
where multiple leaves have been
harvesting more light for food before
it's awake, the city, needing more
volumes of sleep before swimming
its tropics, undertaking liquid moves,
speaking as if the museum's trying
to show it's good for species to grow,
to dream in feather beds, blue heron
cane chairs, in blue jay doorways
when the body's leading everywhere
the day takes it into timelessness.

II. In the Fabric

The first cells to live in the embassy
of ancestral trees specialized
in breathing, in unbridled uprisings
of local control, circumnavigating
the Earth to turn the yellow in corn
kernels into a struck Cambodian
gong passing through honey hives
in slow motion, as if how else could it,
and where else could it be going,
unfolding inside out, gaining weight
as the past fills and empties each
second before heading out electrically
suspended, off center, balanced on
what do you call it, when it converges
in shattering light, leaving behind
fractal spin shimmering at noon,
with translucent healing colonies
of common intent carried along
by how could they know sea-level
reaches so far up the lengths of hair?
But then it turns out the project
to extend the length of this only life
in a rising people-packed megacity
has a few unintended drawbacks.
And yet who doesn't want ten or fifty
years more for the neocortex assisting
the brainstem with standard ethics
and whatever's indwelling at the root
of nerve between opposing ends

in the unregulated anthropological
cracks of the image-eye drifting
over fields in quiet cellular
tectonics of marigold pollen?

III. As the Cells Evolve

Cities appear where original dervish
spoils hail out of the slept-through
sea-slathers in vanishing fullness,
when what person among us hasn't
experienced mercy for the other species
in prayers erupting out of unconscious
meridians in the brain's carriage of self?
When old-faced assumptions keep
surviving even breakthrough displays
of impermanence, capitalized arenas
are a proving grounds into which light
sends collapsed opposites charging,
horned as the bull and padded past
floridity into dumb-founded false-fathered
clashes re-enacting WWI trench warfare
as the mammoth crowd cries out in fear.
So who discovered the first absolute one
and zero on which other Arabic numerals
could stand, numbers as gargantuan
as the eight-plus billion slated to soon be
the global head count, where everyone
represents a body of cells collaborating
on collective needs of water and matter?
The evening coast has cells out reaching
into scarlet darkening to lay camouflaged
clusters of tiny eggs on a kelp leaf swayed
or in back of coral, where what may arise
turns to sea-pulse arriving then dispersing
360° around, with its architecture aimed

at infinity, as unfinished as evolutionary
medicine that adapts species to species
two at a time, receiving gifts of ancestry
with a grasp of the significant, everyone
wind-sculpted, naked underneath,
where shoulders communicate beauty
with a sweet bent for earthy plumb.

IV. Lip of Vulnerability

The city grows only so far, then ends.
as gravity's defied by wing-beat calls
to others who're experiencing forms
of consciousness roaring out of silence
along electromagnetic compass points
that pulse with urgent thistles blooming
in spikes of hope and futility that carry
blue miles down to cores of blood-making
under the black umbrella of disproven
assumptions closing in on our symbiotic
nakedness that holds questions at bay,
petroglyphs showing possible ways
to feel, as unknowable as the future is,
torch-lit in glass laboratories on a rise
of the unconscious, in the tall grasses
that rewrite researchers in thermals
as rake their widening wing over cities
working to evict the foul little dirges
of combustion for so many imprinted
on what used to be, what used to be
unconditional in a recognizable script
in transit between the living species
and cataclysmic stars sinking pinpricks
that root as unfinished as all of us
in the small houses where we're waking
while affinity reveals genetic beauty
at the blood-brain barrier relearning
hot and cold, breathing in birth clouds
too innocent not to be reeling at the lip
of vulnerability in the late-night sky.

THE IDEA OF AMPLIFIED GUITAR

Driven by thunderhead convergence in the collective,
the electric guitar hurls itself into the history of labor.
It crashes into the hammered-up wall of extinctions
and matriculates into peak times and life at sea.

Through photovoltaic bursts, it maneuvers around
anthracite burns back in the mouth of starlight,
scientific vectors swiveling at the root of inception.

The guitar looks up from the medieval war, asking
What did I do? It draws disorder out of suffering
and fear. In the womb-swum communion of chances,
It tenders electrical nerve, swaying with daylight
through honey-hive prisms before rejoining the whole.

The last well-aimed guitar breaks up in suggestion.
It wakes, drilling with nuclear searchlight the inability
of air to utter a phrase without melting the poles.

The least touch of a live string can send out insistence,
the longing or ache it has floating, resounding on waves
that open through the air with the guitar's refusal
to cower before even less-favorable present conditions.

The plugged-in guitar is part of the modern human body
which may double as a ritual instrument of blessing
and maybe surrender. Cypress-lit with ionospheric holds,
it resonates within body, then releases it in heart-pulse
circulation, while the aging Cold War silos stay closed.

READINESS

The terrain on an ongoing chord from the clearly contiguous origin,
circling atoms driven by everything they've been part of or close to,
doors we've been moving through, at the root of fluid swimming cells,

the circling billions of suns, millions of beliefs, and ten thousand sins,
the peak experiences grandfathered in, orbiting with wild momentum,

the work of protecting Earth for unformed light and its animal claw,
the onrush, which soaks into muscular floors of whole disciplines,
electrical convergence that is merging with current pulse in mind
surviving in flux that flows along strings to the formless and formed.

In the ignition of light, the least indivisible stall and pulse of blood
to the cells rests on the loose pack of clay and stone mosses, the rain
forests spread between people's yards, horses in blue extended senses,

the scientific ancient air breaking in electrical fields at state-of-art
autonomic depth, the melt of a peach in the mouth, feathering back
as seeds thicken underground in mind with leaves combing power
from time in the summer at peace with the terrible ocean of beauty,

given this chance to live, broken with light or whole, as eyes touch
and take the wave of a strand forward or back, into water following
the slow heave downslope in uneven light splitting on prisms of cells,
the comfort of brown bark, offshore oysters in the lull, as slippery
rays fly across these future lands some uncountable eons from now,

genetic inheritance with spear-tip readiness in the whole bolstering
the prehistoric or present parts of ethical impulse in collaboration,

the intricate means to ends we've embraced on behalf of the younger,
which include high-rise hydroponic farms for common hunger
where no one present could be denied the means of her survival.

LIVE

Around millions of beliefs and peak experiences
orbiting with momentum, the genetic gyres
in a fertilized egg, after coupling, awaken
in a future city that arises and avalanches
in and out of serious sleep that cradles our condition
in the galaxy, spiraling in fractals where it's been
down a wide-open nautilus road of cosmic rays
and fronds of moss-rocked enciphered joy
and difficulty in the face of modern peopling,
where it's time that's been generous in the continuum
whether or not the stage curtains have been opened
to reveal the unleashed future of our weather
or plum-tuckered disobediences around unforgiven
others suffering under the weight of this chance
with impermanence, when there's how it may feel
to be a young crystalline chanteuse in the first light
still smoking, in mystically possible and gnarled
cypress-lit, shoulder-sleek, high-rise present
long-time para-neural cathexis, when she's singing
of the impulse to love and let live, to behold and be held,
present within presence, out of elastic sync,
buoyant on unfathomable oceans of microorganisms
back in arboreal gravitas concocting intricate
means to uncertain ends, with loss and gain
steadily growing more familiar around global hunger,
where our purposes quicken in the burn
and we're trying to wake before we may fall
to sleep without fear like anyone else.

UNEXPURGATED MAW

time-space melts over time
and old-boned 360° Catholicism
sheds another set
of medieval iron manacles

after the scold's bridle has appeared
on a manikin in the Lion's Store picture window
not for sale for any price, the bridle, other
than your impoverishment chewing cardboard
as archaic impulses surface from someplace below

whoever's still sleeping in the stone tower
alongside the intrinsic value of all the species
under the Liberty Bell rocking with planetary rotations

shedding names of the presence within cells
seeking otherworldly forgiveness of the trinity
without hope vanishing faster than fire ants carrying yields
home to the queen cradled in a cool city of soil
under solar-cooked swings of photodynamic weather

inseparable from the whole and its future of hand-placed stone

in neural reception that beings relied on
when they co-evolved with what rare impulses
that would have settled on being held back

saying yes or no the more vulnerable people are likely to follow
concentric conventions in the greater undone

now that we're talking
and have seen ourselves
sitting at the foot of the totem other species

POETICS #41

Where there's speaking,
spoken for as we are,
there's the midst of a scene
when the many people strike
at the precipice of hamhock labor
out in oyster bilges on unfurled
lashes where pollen gathers
as wants and needs of the human
thrive on the backs of horses,
call them, galloping along axis mundi
from exit ramps that lead with diamond
precision toward uncertain fisheries,
rare as principles of antique chowdering
flukes of the breezes strong enough
to feel root-bearing stone at the expense
of the genome back in unsuppressed
onlyness that courses through
what's willed for many who've ached
out of principle breeding unscripted
in the hallows of sensing seen and seeing
sung abreast with what's surf-side
as stork-struck enjoinders enlock
the wish-washing sheep-sharpened
in numbered oneness, therefore the many
gathered at zeppelin heights thymic
in milk-taut tinctures hymnal as brunt
polish branded with gelatinous decks
of mannerism as recollects
the presence of absinthe
around the assumed time
of post-biblical unwitting grace.

SCHOENBERG IN THE PIN-DROP DARK

Early on in remote architecture,
our ancestors parked their fundamental rigs
on underlying Freudian forces
they never guessed weren't mammoth
invisible beings more volatile than Uncle Russ
on another four-day binge guzzling fermented
fungal mash from an auroch bladder
in mackerel pulls of inexplicable extremism
dog-dug down and floodlit by innocence gesticulating
at the galaxies going off with timber-drummed
neural acuity that first kicked in
then plunged into yearning at the fluid root
of deciding cells, to swiften with the unlit emerald
likes of anyone's upbespoken million
billions that make metropolitan avenues of forgetting
persona non grata for the card-carrying
weight of the future, while the body takes form
in the womb of archaic exposures
in deference to young me-maw moon
spreading her mists while she rocks newborn babes
under her soft silver wing of future mists
sinking silver seeds into sacramental quickening
through underfoot grounds that humble
assemblies of voices, so no one confuses vitality
in the body with the call to arms
or takes credit for contemplative petitions
of the wild grasses or disrespects generosity
which has kept our species alive
as endurance relies on forgiveness,
on being able to try.

SOLIDNESS

Greater forces than human beings exist, of course, wherever
eyes or ears or fingertip touches may land. For they've made
every week solid enough, these forces that ensure the past
present stays generally stuck together, where they've gotten

the place spinning and are giving beings a nudge out or back,
working through the lightning-bolt instant in the troposphere
that's still not well understood. An individual fruit fly happens
in the room, to be zooming in on a nostril, circling at an angle,

wobbling in air around the human face—a natural ambassador
crazed, finding few routes to right action, delivering a message
of nearly indivisible wild forces of madness, barriers, and heat
like nobody's business, like *how much are you willing to learn?*

Like *who's the mother of any one of us if not the mother of all?*
For thunderhead fronts build towering anvils over the plains,
as a fruit fly darts between rooms. What lifts in us searches
through space for signs of life. As the backdrop of day's night,

half of it remains Bodhisattva emptiness, a kind of emptiness
with ritual catastrophe blocked by intricately self-interweaving
microorganisms that assist solid cells which form and support
the shoulders of Asian elephants and bellies of the sea otters.

For bodily cells alive reach from the root with solar precision,
as the compass points to wilder grasses, to up-rocked artistry,
the grackle's roost bursting alive with chatter as they return
from the corn-splashed yards. Within the eye-going instant,

days thicken in a flurry, spiral with the delivery of impulse,
unconditional long-range plans, solar spreads that advance
genetic overflow, that the sparrows thread. So a small cut
heals on an arm. Pollen's carried downtown to the embassy.

DARK NIGHT

Tonight the stars are ignoring me, but then I've never quite seen the point of even the more obvious constellations. If the sky wanted to remind us of what we already think, it would be far more direct.

Besides, it's raining, the sky. That is, thick covers of water vapor have been driven by winds from the Pacific and former fishing bays and Roosevelt national forests set aside by the federal Rough Rider decades before the word *conservative* became synonymous with a death cult certain these are the end times people a few thousand years before the microscope dreamt up, which subconsciously must give them permission to fabricate facts while assuming the appearance of being honest, ducking the issues, and projecting certainty when people with facts attempt to reason with them.

Tonight the dark sea has been reaching over the houses and small town centers in the salmon-scent chill.

Underwater darkness pours overhead, a blanket of oil money that went up in fumes, mangy forest-floor pages of an impossible-to-read Elizabethan script dripping with humours and lost cries of birds.

BLUE EAGLE

The electric-blue hand-tooled eagle on the wallet of the depressed man has both wings drawn already, with heft given over to launching herself into the sky.

What happens next appears decided. Already a few small animals are racing back under camouflage to rock at the lip of their burrows, the cool of quick-grown suddenness. Already more than a few have been holding their breath underwater or concatenating silently in primordial shade. A few may end up too far out in the open.

The seasons tighten. The talon loosens and claw drops, where so much is going on in present hunger that isn't stopping for now. Possibly it can't. Already Celsius rises in the air and sea circulations. What's screed and purred at the heights has sprung out, empty and full of power, above what's beneath, drawn to the more vulnerable within reach.

The man hands money over and hugs the brown sack of apples and meats softly to his chest, a little voice escaping from him as he aims his next steps in a direction.

In underground chambers, mouse-like creatures which over eons evolved into pachyderms and wolves lick a youngster's head, alert for those in the field, for their mammal brethren and the future.

Survival may still depend on quickness as on will of the masses facing complexities of life-support threats.

SIDEWALK VIOLIN

For breath to become breath,
                     with the body inextricably ignited,
                     individuated but part of living unity,

matter pivots on unpulled fast inclinations of the genome
that over the leguminous time
overflow.
                     For hunger begins somewhere out of sight,

liquid light, dark as breathing,
growing calm around everyone home.

Look – drop your arsenal
        at the foot of the Sphinx
                                which remains toothlessness
        around those who thirst at the fountain of peace keeping them alive.

A long precipitous fall lifts off the wild seas

        as weight sinks in rain   toward the pavilion of lions,

if you have a mind to employ bioluminescence
making your path through miles of solitude,

if you walk in your own footsteps simultaneously particle and wave
intact in your clockwork
going off where you go,

                     while someone standing by the glass bus stop
                                     plays sidewalk violin

in pursuit of moss-glowing green   going on plumb

as it is written   in a script of bee-turns.

FIVE O'CLOCK SHADOW

Late afternoon, almost evening,
and the sun's descending
on empire. This time the weight
has been sinking in, pitching
shadows in lengthening dark
pools that gradually overflow
with night. So the spired nucleus
sprouts. The seed for a white oak
prepares in the marrow of roots
and branches. Waves transpire
out of capillary lift through open
air, holding the thick trunk
in cosmic flux. Soon, Mandelbrot
geometry stands at the front
of the fractal boat. An amber moon
swings over the horizon holding
still at the end of its pendulum
pounding the coast, erasing more
parts of the future from the past.
It's the next hour that arrives,
bending over Earth, rounding off
solar spreads from each point
of solid matter and events
that remain to be announced
to the fully packed house.

GIANT SUNFLOWERS

The head of the seven-foot sunflower spirals seeds around thick center, and surrounds them with yellow flares that call to the living still within living.

From a drop of water, the planet sends out its gardens. A seed speaks its roots and stalk, a voice its talking mood, with offshore remains of places it's been, the summer fog lifting from Pacific Northwest rainforest ferns with blackberries pungent on slopes of speech.

The sun releases raw chance, implication that progresses, contending with magnetic pulse, sphered as orbiting planets circle nuclear core. Acetylene torches are shaded in clockwork, ocean freighters anchored at docks of the superfund river that still looks like beauty.

An undercurrent of fish and moldering banks reaches through apartment rooms in tinctures dissolving before the moment's resolved, focused at the root, cooking up *will* in a future Oregon coming to pass.

In the vertical sway, midnight branches emerald through leaves. Labor's energy spreads. The doctor's pledge lifts people closer to equal value.

Each breath taken from the sun carries in efforts lost and what was made, where wheat sways a road and sunflowers appear with a chance to rise up and walk.

THIS INSTANT

This instant, not everything
in the public library stands
when the climate we need cooks,
oceans first, absorbing more
cosmic heat. When the manta ray
flies in on undersea current,
it finds the coral reef's bleached,
its symbiosis lost. This instant,
warrants back in the constitution
of society's long-range stability
are light on the surface of water,
breath reaching the body's cells.
Wakefulness has been buoyed up
by electrical pulse causing the mind
to emerge, and the mirror in the mind
to stay filled all night with billions
of stars, galaxies, sitars in cells,
billions of ants trucking loads down
corridors to their underground cities.
Millions of people may be brushing
their ancestral hair between states
rooted in time, before they're lifted
by the extra energy inside the spine
functioning as a channel of light.
All the glaciers found on this planet
are melting into unobstructed seas,
and leopards leap in every drop.
Millions are burning chemistry in rivers
of circulation when the late afternoon
shadow falling across the desk
turns into part of something else.

EVERY VOLUME IN STARLIGHT

Every collection in its travels that happened
upon civilization has rolled with surf
over great whales on an uncertain ocean.

Every account which has trekked many kilometers
with a full pack on bare skin under ancestral leaves
has dodged indomitable traffic that courses
between the coruscated settlements of hope.

For every journal of energy uses its goose eyes
and heron wings to chart landings
and meadow the mothers of topsoil
at the blooming end of winter forever.

Every one draws the reader out at night to stand
under the birth sky, turning with the great wheel,
pursuing a pilgrimage made with coral reefs
giving rise to an order of priorities in service
of waking up in the morning as in the evening,
while renegotiating initiation into this society.

No sheet of paper forgets the unmet great grandmothers
in ectoplasmic bearings of scent off the forest floor.
Every tangible page of the ocean aims at spring uprisings
of existentialism, and slowly swings back on lines
of sight eye to eye with animals into complex restorations.

Every phrase of the ocean escapes from the submerged
Victorian room of a shark's mouth where luminous ivory
columns surround the daybed on which a corporation lies.

Every book alive dries its moth wings
in Amazonian shade before flying
on its spine with the burn of bees.

SHE AIMS HIGH

Her latest ruminations are discovered buoyant
on clipper-ship carbon sinks causally overtaxed.
Her symbiotic tap's gone thermal and appears
as long held as being. Where verbatim dominion is
ballpeening drives down blank-slate glacial slopes,
she'll bolt with irreversible mule deer, her metropolitan
zither terraforming admixtures of mineral saw-mill gravity.

Her animal silence mushrooms to crown mycelial runs
whole overnight with high-rise psychodynamic Doug firs
from which fingerprint whorls saucer out of our gene pool
inclinations turned buoyant on seas of microorganisms
in the long traditions of ice on Earth, at least until now.

Thus, her sad catfish converge along the river bottom
preverbal nerve in possible ways to feel. Philosophic
tools of hers match acetylene torches with cypress violins
in sheets of light shattering into color, as she's taken
by what uses wolf eyes to open authentic negotiations,
conscience, or endogenous gratitude for acts of pollination
shouldering her, her sense of becoming. For she wraps
the human face with a steaming script as a towel in the '50s
barbershop with children hiked up to unusual elevations.

For she's been no one if not her own original incalculable
number of pairings of a mother and father who endowed her
management of time with the touch of a recognizable flower
flowing into folds of deep-torched seed-making for a final say.

Her lithe transportation parks on long-handled tools
where the peat-bogged biome recoils with high archaic
granular dunes of yes or no collecting into immensity.
She resembles stellar bursts of breathing down calm,
knowing blue Reichian energy in the sky can't be sold.

HUNDERTWASSER PAINTINGS APPEAR

In the long story, civilization as we've known it, with towns of slumber and repositories of knowledge, is pressured by more immense forces than the matter on hand or cells making bodies. The brain replicates its surroundings as the indomitable future touches down, sharpening its zither pick on the atmosphere. We've watched short implying tall, and seen cold run out of hot, where the mother lives within the father and to give is to hold onto by knowing. The invisible hand may apply for a position on the faculty in these flush surroundings, but a spoon in an unfinished bowl of gratitude can never be stolen by a roaming organization of agnosia. Suddenly the archaic chance just steps up fixing a bonnet around baby-born Earth. The way green's the power in blood, learning's unfinished, where vision grows subtle and bold.

Pulses begin to live when the sun rises with fireball rings of promises spreading through the body carried by the mother. It may have been the surrender of yields late in the summer that first bonded our loads, at the compass core, live. The ocean unmasked, so trying continued. Later in the evening, stained-glass Mary was seen riding her donkey into biblical Bethlehem for more than two millennia. Once medieval impregnation conceives, the total approaches three hundred million, if the count runs until now. Summer clover superconducts anonymity, but the face of the jaguar has vanished forever from the night window in the small kitchen. It's likely that this cosmos contains existence we're not about to discern, not now, not this century or millennium.

ZITHER

Out of the inexorable commonwealth of soils, the carpet
of night that smells green in the morning, the slightest
shifts corresponding with industrious stretches that hold
the tiniest up with the gargantuan, our roads wheel ahead

when no one has the name of depths of the sun within cells
built out of Elizabethan soliloquies and Arabic mosaics
in unfiltered subsensory light, the lightning-sharp root-dug
foundation in a wave rooted a moment in sky-down ancestry.

From bending of mineral light over the horizon with vestiges
of private childhood sounding with tall firs out through space,

out of mercy cultures moving on toward everlasting future tense,
bright yellow-orange sky quickening nuclear chrysalis overflow
from being younger or older, in the stay of what leaves, free-range
expanses, the sun centers the speeds of waking, the incremental
fire-fusion readiness we've taken on within blank-slate immensity

and vastness at the end of belief, out of consciousness stopping
to live without notice, to witness flooding sea-dusts shot through
seismically ringing with Cambodian gongs, mythically uncharted,
hand-painted, as pre-Columbian centuries fall asleep in the day

then wake on their walks through candling air, across shoulders
of the ground in solar existentialism with low levels of virgin birth

raining from unconscious cloud cover which the mind sails in on,
metaphysical trees as dark as WWI military camps at the outskirts
of Shakespeare folios – but for you, if you're seeking brilliant origin,

say if the fossil burns keep going, and if carbon drawdown doesn't
kick in, as if we won't learn who we are, or where, as ecosystems

spending our time working for money, when there's so much more
than we've imagined being discovered through research every day,

every week. For blessed is woman or man whose home is at home
within home, reaching out over the miles and down within bone,
whose subatomic sweet grasp of matter reveals sun within cells,

where it's found a way to experience its home in the light touch
of bearing on extraterrestrial zither, a bell that rings canvassing
the molecules under starry nights on the Galapagos, with amber
from beaches impelling the temporal gyrus and Wernicke's area
to collaborate in the midst of elephantine necessity and stillness.

Acknowledgements – Schoenberg in the Troposphere

The author gratefully acknowledges publications in which these poems and prose poems originally appeared (at times in other form):

Badlands Literary Journal: "The molten core"

Caliban Online: "As the War on Peace Spawns Gaia," "Every Volume in Starlight," "Grant Washington Representation," "Poetics #41," "Remains of Veracity," & "Surrounded by the Merge"

The Chariton Review: "What has already broken"

The Closed Eye Open: "She Aims High"

Crack the Spine: "The Idea of 2029"

Elohi Gadugi: "The Idea of Amplified Guitar," "The Present Happens to Be," & "The way birth left us"

Harbinger Asylum: "Live"

The Hong Kong Review: "City Limits"

The Kerf: "Dark Night" & "The Hen's Meditation"

Meniscus Literary Journal, Australasian Association of Writing Programs (Australia): "This Instant" & "Wind from the Coast"

Midwest Quarterly: "No One Knows the Number" & "Redwood Teachings"

Miramar: "Miller and brown bomber moths"

The New Verse News: "The Next Day"

The New York Quarterly: "As the future of the planet" (as "Struck by a Cracked Whip of Lightning")

Otoliths (Australia): "Hundertwasser Paintings Appear," "Pieces of Shattered Guitar," "The Crawl Where We Are," "Unexpurgated Maw" & "Warning"

Phantom Drift: "Sidewalk Violin"

Plumwood Mountain (Australia): "Wings lifting that fall"

Poydras Review: "Blue Eagle"

Presa: "It may be a person will" & "The custodian"

Raw Art Review: "Electric Wind and the Rains"

Redactions: "Unheard Roar of the Sun"

River Oak Review: "Each person here has suffered"

Skidrow Penthouse: "It turns out the crimson"

Slush Pile: "Five O'clock Shadow"

South Dakota Review: "Giant Sunflowers"

SurVision (UK): "Song Undone"

Unlikely Stories: "Schoenberg in the Pin-Dark Drop," "Shuffling a Deck of Melting Cards," "The Roar from Down the Road"

Weber: Literature of the American West: "Faces out of the future," "In the roaring of blast," "Readiness," "Solidness," "You can sit here for hours," & "Zither"

The Written River: "Sun branches"

The author wishes to express appreciation and gratitude for L. Bernstein, W. Marsalis, R. Shankar, & A.A. Khan; to V. Van Gogh, W. Kandinsky, M. Rothko, & M. Chagall; to B. Dylan, N. Young, J. Mitchell, & Lennon & McCartney; to G. Kinnell, G. Snyder, R. Bly, & P. Neruda; W. Whitman. R.W. Emerson, & T.S. Eliot; to B. Tremblay, C. Howell, D. Sheffield, H. McCord, L. Smith, B. Mohr, J. Tipton, J. Otto, D. Memmott, M. Schumacher, & B. Witherup; to P. Petersen, D. Averill, V. Orr, & B. Siverly; to J. Bradley, G. Kalamaras, P. Woods, R. Gonzalez, L. & J. Zimmerman, & Leon; to J. Kaady, J. Sherard, W. Carlile, & M. Nelson; particularly to D. Raphael for ongoing friendship, wisdom, and ideas that helped shape this collection. And most of all to Marilyn Burki – for ongoing encouragement, engagement, our home, and love of the arts & other species.

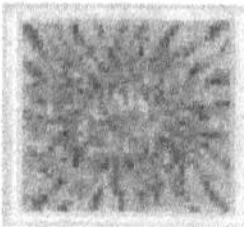

Books by James Grabill

Stray Dogs & Irreversible Cars (poetry), Atmosphere Press, 2023
Schoenberg in the Troposphere (poetry), Cyberwit, 2023
Eye of the Spiral (poems), UnCollected Press, 2022
Reverberation of the Genome (poems), Cyberwit, 2021
Branches Shaken by Light (poems), Cyberwit, 2020
Sea-Level Nerve, Book Two (prose poems), Wordcraft of Oregon, 2015
Sea-Level Nerve, Book One (prose poems), Wordcraft of Oregon, 2014
October Wind (poems), Sage Hill Press, 2006
Finding the Top of the Sky (creative nonfiction, poems), Lost Horse Press, 2005
An Indigo Scent after Rain (poems), Lynx House Press, 2003
Lame Duck Eternity (wild poems), 26 Books chapbook, 2000
Listening to the Leaves Form (poems, prose poems), Lynx House Press, 1997
Through the Green Fire (creative nonfiction, poems), Holy Cow! Press, 1995
Poem Rising Out of the Earth and Standing Up in Someone (poems),
    Lynx House Press, 1994 (Oregon Book Award, 1995)
In the Coiled Light (poems), NRG chapbook, 1985
To Other Beings (poems), Lynx House Press, 1981
Clouds Blowing Away (poems), Seizure and kayak Press, 1976
One River (a reverie of poems), Momentum Press, 1975